Daniel Atwood

REVEALING
the Secrets of
LEADERSHIP

A Hands-On Guide
for Teaching Basic Principles

ISBN: 1439224102
ISBN-13: 9781439224106

This book will give you an outline for teaching positive leadership to anyone of any age in any organization. My approach is coming from the perspective of a high school music educator. In this book you will see references to how this applies to the music classroom, but upon closer examination you will find that these principles of leadership can be applied to any organization and to any age level no matter where these individuals may be in their pursuit of positive leadership.

My hope is that this manual will help you to develop a strategy for constructing a leadership workshop, which you can lead, that will utilize seven principles, thought provoking questions, and hands-on activities to better equip your students in becoming a positive force in your organization.

This manual has been tried and tested with my own students. I have been using this method for the past five years, and what a difference it has made in our band program! Students understand what is expected from the student leaders, they are given ample opportunity to demonstrate what they have learned, and are able to put their leadership skills to use on a daily basis.

I hope you find as much success using this manual with your students as I have had using it with mine.

REVEALING THE SECRETS OF LEADERSHIP

Finding a manual that helps teach leadership is a very difficult task, yet student leadership is an integral part of what we should be teaching as educators. I have chosen to construct a manual, which will lay out a process for teaching leadership concepts to students. In my research, I deal with seven principles of effective positive leadership. I have researched philosophies and beliefs from many sources as to what positive leadership consists of, and synthesized them into what I am calling the SECRETS of student leadership. These seven principles are as follows:

- Sensitivity
- Enthusiasm
- Communication
- Respect
- Effectiveness
- Trustworthiness
- Selflessness

The resulting manual discusses each principle and contains quotes cited from various sources supporting the importance of teaching these principles.

Introduction

In my pursuit to help my students develop I have found there to be a lack of teacher-friendly resources available for music educators on the subject of student leadership. While there are many leadership books available that relate to the corporate or business world, it is difficult to find a manual or course of study, which can be easily used to effectively teach these principles to young people. In the world of music education we often put our students in positions of authority where we expect them to take control of situations and lead the rest of the ensemble in a positive direction. When these students, who we thought would be good leaders, fall short of our expectations, we as adults become upset or discouraged. We may even accuse the child of not living up to his/her potential, but perhaps the problem does not rest with the student. The fault may in fact rest with the person who put the child in that position. Do we educate the student as to what we expect from our student leaders? All too often we put a child in a leadership position, but we never teach them how to be a positive leader.

When I first came to the realization that I was putting my students in this position, I decided at that moment to pursue developing this guide for others. I began to research what it takes to be a positive leader. I also wanted to become involved in other programs that have leadership as one of the components of its overall purpose.

Many of us have experienced music teachers who use music as the means and the ends by which they teach. In that type of classroom music is the main priority. The goal and the focus of the program are to produce the highest quality music. As is often the case, the high quality of music comes at much too costly a price. The director may ultimately get what they want, but it is at the expense of the student. In my classroom I decided I want to make music the means by which I teach a greater end. I want to use lessons in music to produce better quality citizens.

As I began my research and became more involved in community and civic organizations, it soon became apparent to me that there are two central questions when dealing with the issue of leadership, and that these questions must be answered before we can continue to investigate this topic: "What is leadership?" and "Can leadership be taught?" In order to answer these questions first leadership must be defined, and then an inquiry must be made as to whether or not it can be taught.

What is Leadership?

It is my position that if ten people were gathered and asked to define leadership, more than likely there would be ten different responses given. When I asked this question of my own students I had responses like: "It's being in charge..." "Leadership is getting people to do what you want them to do..." and "Leadership is making others do the work for you." So, how does one define leadership? Most people would agree that leadership deals with one's ability to get others to follow. The question then becomes, how does one get people to follow? Simply put, we must make use of influence. Maxwell (1998) stated the following:

> Princess Dianna has been characterized in many ways. But one word that I've never heard used to describe her is *leader*. Yet that's what she was. Ultimately, she made things happen because she was an influencer, and leadership is influence-nothing more, nothing less (p. 13).

So according to Maxwell leadership is influence. Influence stems from the effect that we have on other people, and this can come in two forms. Leaders can have a positive influence or a negative influence on others. This coincides with the two types of leadership which is why this definition is very fitting.

Our modern society is very familiar with the power of negative influence and leadership. One simply mentions the names Osama Bin Laden, Saddam Hussein, or Adolf Hitler, and people will grasp the concepts of negative influence and negative leadership rather easily. These men came to power through the influence they had on other individuals and on the general populace of their nations. So how did they do it? The oversimplified answer is that they had to develop their abilities to influence others. They learned how to have influence.

Can Leadership Be Taught?

    If the agreement is made that leadership is influence, then the question becomes more defined. Can we be taught how to have an influence on others? The answer to this question is a definitive yes. One can be taught how to influence other people. The term "born leader" is often used to describe people, and this is why the question of innate ability versus learned behaviors exists when talking about the subject of leadership. All of us are born with the potential to have some type of influence on the lives of those around us. In fact every person that ever lived had an impact on someone. Maxwell (1993) acknowledged, "Sociologists tell us that even the most introverted individual will influence ten thousand other people during his or her lifetime" (p. 2)!

    "Leadership is not an exclusive club for those who were 'born with it.' The traits that are the raw materials of leadership can be acquired. Link them up with desire and nothing can keep you from becoming a leader" (Maxwell, 1993, Leadership can be taught, p 1). The "raw materials" that Maxwell refers to in the previous quote provide what will comprise the majority of this manual. What are those raw materials? These are the various traits and principles of leadership that can be taught to those who desire to become a positive force in any organization. That's right. These traits will help anyone in any organization. This is why it is so important to me to use my music classroom and its subject matter to teach a higher goal.

Method

I have taken information from several sources and developed what I am calling the SECRETS of leadership. The word secrets will be used as an acronym for those characteristics and principals.

In this manual I will walk through each step of the process of putting together a presentation for your students on the subject of leadership. Each topic in the word "SE-CRETS" has an activity to go along with it. After a rationalization about the importance of each topic the activity will be explained.

I usually begin each workshop by introducing myself as not only a leadership clinician, but also as a world famous magician. I then perform a simple magic trick or two. Any magic trick will work as I have done card tricks, coin tricks and "mind reading." Once the students are amazed by my feats of prestidigitation, I ask them if they think I posses some sort of magical powers? Of course the answer is "no." I confirm their belief and explain that I possess no magical powers, I simply know a secret which they don't know. I then tell them I am not going to reveal secrets of magic to them today, but I am going to reveal secrets of leadership.

My hope is that you will take this manual and use it to develop a leadership training program for your students. Giving anyone, especially young people, the ability to develop and grow into a confident positive leader has benefits far beyond what we can comprehend. If you follow this plan, continue to reinforce these ideas throughout the year and affirm when your students do what is right by making admirable choices, I am sure you will see immediate benefits in your program as well. So let us look at the SE-CRETS of student leadership.

Sensitivity

In order to be a positive leader, one must be sensitive in his or her thoughts and actions. As a teacher one has a tremendous responsibility to his/her students. One must provide a model of personal strength and character that will benefit his/her students when those students leave the safety and security of their programs. Mullins (1985) illustrated this by saying the following:

> Does this mean we have to go around with a constant smile on our faces? Do we have to talk rapidly and walk with a lively pace, eyes shining brightly, enjoying a never-ending high energy level? Of course not. As teachers we will have mood swings just as everyone else does. Some days will be difficult, downright unpleasant, and we will get through them as best we can. Trying to conceal these low points is a waste of time because students know how to read our behavior with uncanny accuracy, easily spotting phoney [sic] actions and words. Students respect teachers who act like human beings and seldom expect perfection from us (p. 33).

Being sensitive to one's own mood and feelings will help improve interactions with others. Students understand that their teachers are not perfect, and that even teachers have bad days. When this occurs the educator is provided with an incredible teaching opportunity. It is at this point that the teacher can model how to behave in a constructive and productive manner, rather than allowing an imperfect situation to effect the way others are being treated. Often times in these situations people do the opposite. We all know people who allow their bad mood to have an adverse effect on those around them.

Outstanding leaders are not only aware of their own feelings but they are sensitive to the multitude of differences that exist within the organization, are able to see past those differences and strive to inspire all members to do their best. These differences may include race, religion, social status, socio-economic status, learning styles, and countless other orientations. If you as a leader can unify your groups, despite their many differences, you will be able to take your organization to new heights.

Dr. Tim Lautzenheiser (1993) a well-known and respected clinician on student leadership said:

> We all have had the experience of working with an extraordinary teacher, and when we are in the presence of such a person we reach beyond our known limits and discover we can perform at a higher level. In truth, the newfound talents and abilities were always within us, but the master teacher triggered something which catapulted us (the student/learner) to the next level. The mentor not only served as a role model, but also imparted valuable knowledge which helped unlock more of our human potential (p. 33).

In order for us to be strong positive leaders and have influence on the members of our organizations sensitivity is a must. This does not mean that the leader must agree with or even understand all of the difference that exist, but he or she must be willing to accept the members for who they are, and strive to inspire them to achieve their maximum potential.

Sensitivity Activity:

Begin by saying, "We all like cartoons right? Well, we are going to begin with a short video by Dr. Seuss. As you watch this I want you to think about your feelings toward the various characters in this cartoon, and when the video is over we are going to discuss this." Then show "The Sneetches" from the video "Dr Seuss-Green Eggs and Ham and Other Favorites." This video is distributed by Universal Studios, and can be purchased through almost any video dealer or online.

After watching the video talk with the students using the following discussion questions:

- As you watched the video, what were your feelings toward the Sneetches without stars?
- As you watched the video, what were your feelings toward the Sneetches with stars?

The preceding two questions deal directly with sensitivity. This will tell you which students are not only sensitive to the feelings of others, but it can also tell you if students are sensitive to the potential that others possess. In order to investigate this further ask the following:

- Are the star-bellied Sneetches better than those without stars?
- Do they communicate better, or perform better?
- So if the answer is no, then why do the star-bellied Sneetches think they are better?

At this point you may want to remind the students of the scene where the parent Sneetch tells the younger Sneetch that we don't associate with that kind of Sneetch. In short, it's what the Sneetches teaches. Then discuss the following points:

- Do we do that as human beings? (discuss hatred/discrimination based on race, religion, sexual orientation and other facets of society)
- Do we do that in our own school or this organization? (jock vs music nerds, preps vs goths, seniors vs freshmen, brass vs percussion, etc.)

Conclude this activity by asking the students to take five minutes and write down a time when they discriminated against someone or were discriminated against, and to then come up with the correct way the situation should have been handled. Share these on a volunteer basis, and end the activity by talking to them about recognizing when this occurs in our organization. Get thoughts on what the students think they could do to help when a situation like this occurs. You may want to discuss having the courage to step in and stop it. This is not only hard to do in society ("in the real world"), but it is hard to do here, too.

Enthusiasm

The next component of leadership is enthusiasm. Enthusiasm in this context is not to be misconstrued as being a cheerleader for the group, but rather it should be associated with being a person of passion. Strong leaders, both positive and negative, must possess a passion for their purpose. As an advisor or educator, you must show your passion to your students. They should see your passion for your subject area, your passion for life and your passion for helping them to become better human beings.

Goldman hit on this issue when he talked about securing a conductor for new bands. Goldman (1916) said, "But it is not always the great and learned musician who makes the best conductor, for such a one is often lacking in other essentials, and is sometimes very impractical" (p. 19). One of the "other essentials" Goldman refers to, in my opinion, is passion. The best person for a job may not always be the person who is extremely gifted intellectually or technically. It is often not a question of how much one knows or how skilled an individual is, but it is a question of how much one believes in and cares for the goal. In other words success as a leader is dependent on how passionate the individual is about their purpose.

Passion towards an accomplishment is the driving force for change. Without passion one is simply going through the motions. There is no feeling or emotion behind what they do. It is easy for us to observe when one begins to undertake a task, but has no interest or personal investment in their work. Dr. Peter Boonshaft closely relates passion with emotion. Boonshaft (2002) stated:

> It seems to me the trend over the past few years is for conductors to be more dispassionate. There are many who preach that emotion from the podium is to be avoided. In some circles the word emotion has become a four-letter word. Have we become so concerned about correctness as to be emotionally aloof?

Though we are all entitled to our opinion, I have always lived by the words of George Wilhelm Friedrich Hegel who wrote, "We may affirm absolutely that nothing great in the world has been accomplished without passion" (p. 142).

Can we teach students to have passion? No. I do not think passion is something that can be taught. However, passion is something that can be inspired in students. Through the display of their own passions, educators can inspire that same passion in their students.

One easy way to spark the passion for learning is when an educator infuses their own passion by taking a more inquisitive approach to a subject. This is a very powerful form of influence. As the educator throws out bits of knowledge or fun activities that pertain to the subject, students become more intrigued, and in turn develop a passion for wanting to not only know more, but do more.

Positive feedback from the instructor, peers and parents can go a long way in inspiring enthusiasm in students. Most educators have found that giving words of encouragement in a positive manner inspire students to do more than if we come down hard on them, or belittle them in front of their classmates. Try to give more positive feedback in a day then negative.

The activity that helps the students understand the power of positive feedback comes from Brian Cole Miller (2004) and is called "Kudos."

Enthusiasm Activity:

You will need several Kudos candy bars. In small groups give one to every student. This seems to be more effective if everyone is involved. If dealing with a large group however, ask for a small group of people that know each other fairly well to volunteer to help with this exercise. Stress the fact that they don't need to be friends, they just have to work with each other pretty regularly.

- First pass out one Kudos bar to each participant, and make sure everyone knows the meaning of the word kudos.
- Explain that the candy bar is to be given to someone in order to recognize something they have accomplished or helped with.
- When giving the candy bar, the giver must provide a brief and specific explanation of why the candy bar is being given to that person.
- You go first and give the first Kudos to a participant. (In a group that you are unfamiliar with give Kudos for how attentive a person has been during the workshop, or for consistently providing an encouraging smile.)
- Initiate applause after each Kudos is given
- Be sure to stress that the person being given a Kudos candy bar does not have to go next. The participation in giving Kudos should be completely voluntary.

After you have finished giving kudos to each other, give a Kudos bar to each of the participants for volunteering to help with the activity. Then discuss the following questions:

- How difficult was it to give kudos to someone else? Or was it easy?
- What made it easy or difficult to do?
- How does kudos from your peers differ from kudos from parents or teachers?

Generally speaking students will respond to this last question by stating that kudos from peers tends to mean more to them than it does coming from a teacher. Discuss why that is, and impress upon the students what a positive force they can be in this organization by simply giving positive feedback. Giving kudos to one's peers and to one's students can be a great force in inspiring enthusiasm.

Enthusiasm Activity number two:

Here is another simple activity that works wonders in inspiring positive feed back. It is simply called "Warm Fuzzies." We all know that when we get that "warm fuzzy" feeling it means that we are feeling good about something. This activity encourages students to give each other "warm fuzzy" feelings.

- Have your students cut two pieces of yarn one should be about ten to fifteen feet in length and the other should be long enough to make a necklace. (The yarn can be different colors or the same colors. Leave that up to the students.)
- Have the students loosely wrap the longer piece of yarn around their four outstretched fingers.
- Then slide this off of their fingers and tie one end of the shorter piece around the center of the entire loop that was created with the longer piece.
- Next tie the remaining end of the shorter piece to the ball of yarn creating a necklace.
- Finally use scissors to cut the loops leaving several two to three inch pieces of yarn tied to the end of the necklace.
- These two to three inch pieces can be pulled out of the ball on the end.

Discuss with your students what "warm fuzzy" feelings mean, and talk again about the powerful influence they can have on others by simply providing positive reinforcement. Then once the "warm fuzzy necklaces" are made explain to them that each student is to extend a positive comment to another student. When this is done remove one of the pieces of yarn from your necklace and tie it onto the necklace of the person who received your compliment. Be sure to emphasize that the comments should be truthful and meaningful. They should not be shallow or superficial.

It is best if this activity is done at the beginning of your presentation. Then students may give each other warm fuzzies throughout the day, or try using this activity for an entire week of band camp. You will find that it truly promotes a positive and productive team atmosphere.

Communication

The third principle of leadership that students need to gain an understanding for is communication. When one thinks about communication, talking immediately comes to mind. While this is an important form of communication, it is not the only form. Stephen Covey (1989) believes there are four forms of communication. He said, "Reading and writing are both forms of communication. So are speaking and listening" (p. 237). Some may question listening as a form of communication. Many people think about how to influence others through the spoken word, but most never consider the fact that effective listening can influence others as well. How does effective listening benefit leaders?

As a leader one has to deal with problems that arise in the organization. One common problem that leaders encounter is dealing with those who seem to do nothing but complain. Dale Carnegie refers to this type of person as the "chronic kicker." In his book he discusses how to win friends and influence people. Carnegie (1936) states, "The chronic kicker, even the most violent critic, will frequently soften and be subdued in the presence of a patient, sympathetic listener-a listener who will be silent while the irate fault-finder dilates like a king cobra and spews the poison out of his system" (p. 88). Simply listening to someone, hearing them out, will often calm the person down enough to move forward and find a solution to the problem.

Brinkman and Kirschner (2002) say that most people want to be heard and understood. They go on to say:

> But when two or more people want to be heard and understood at the same time, and no one is willing to listen and understand, an argument or exit is almost inevitable. For this reason, a masterful communicator makes it his or her goal to listen and understand first, before attempting to be heard and understood (p. 41).

If we want our leaders to become masterful communicators, we must impress upon them the importance of listening to others. Listening is not just hearing and offering advice. Effective listening involves undivided attention to what is being said and not interrupting with our own thoughts and suggestions.

Communication Activity:

To demonstrate this type of communication, use the following activity by Tom Jackson (1993). The activity is called "How Bad Can You Be," and is done in the following manner:

- First have a large marker, a roll of tape and a large piece of paper ready.
- Break the students into groups of four, six or eight depending on the size of your group. (Always be sure you have even numbers in your groups.)
- Have each group create a list of what they feel are good listening skills, and write this list on their sheet of paper.
- Once the groups are finished tape each groups list to the wall, and have a representative from each group read their list out loud. (Be sure the groups are practicing effective listening skills during this time.)
- After each group has read their list go back and mark the skills that were named repeatedly. (Circle, underline or place a star next to them.)
- Now, have each of the smaller groups break into couples.
- Have them decide which student will be a speaker and which will be a listener.
- The speaker must tell a story of a recent vacation, events of the day or any other story they would like to tell.
- While the speaker tells their story the listener will demonstrate poor listening skills. (Do the opposite of what was listed.)
- After about one minute have the students reverse roles.

To conclude the activity, look at the following points of discussion:
- How did you feel when you were telling the story to a listener that was not attentive?
- Did you feel differently when you were displaying poor listening skills?
- What should good listeners do? (look at the person talking, don't interrupt, don't respond with anything more than a smile or nod of your head, etc.)

Discuss situations that may arise in your organization where your student leaders may have to practice effective listening. Be sure to emphasize the fact that listening does not mean that you must give any advice. Listening is simply listening, not talking. I am reminded of a poster I once saw in a teacher's classroom that said, "It is no coincidence that the same letters are used to spell LISTEN and SILENT."

Respect

The fourth aspect for consideration in positive leadership is respect. Leaders must respect those whom they are leading. One way to show this respect is to acknowledge when something is being done well. Many "leaders" are very quick to point out mistakes when they occur, but are not as quick to point out when something good happens. Rathe and Clifton (2004) cite recent poll results. "One poll found that an astounding 65% of Americans reported receiving no recognition for good work in the past year" (p. 39).

Constructive criticism is good, but one must be sure to be constructive and not get what they want at the expense of others. Lautzenheiser (1993) explains why berating someone is not a good idea:

> A student leader who chides or berates another student because he or she cannot perform at the expected level or does not meet up to the talents of the "leader" is doing nothing to help the situation. It is less threatening for the subject of such chiding to withdraw than it is for that student to try again and not succeed (p. 149).

If we, as music teachers, want to keep our students involved and fully participating in our programs, it stands to reason that this type of chiding and berating would evoke the converse response from our students. The way to inspire students to stay engaged in the program is by providing positive feedback.

Showing appreciation by recognizing the good that people do will help to create success in organizations, but this appreciation must be sincere and cannot be done in hopes that the giver of this appreciation will get something in return. Carnegie (1936) said:

> If we are so completely selfish that we can't radiate a little happiness and pass on a bit of honest appreciation without trying to get something out of the other

person in return-if our souls are no bigger than sour crab apples, we shall meet with the failure we so richly deserve (p. 100).

At this point talk to the students about how we as leaders sometimes say things that are perceived as being disrespectful when that is not the intention at all. One little word can cause a person to feel as though their thoughts, actions and even appearance are being discounted or belittled. That one little word is "but." When a member of our organization comes up with an idea leaders will often have more to add to that idea. The typical response will sound something like this, "That's a good idea, but if we do this it will be better." The participant in the organization now feels as if their thoughts and ideas are not being considered and that the leader does not respect their feelings and insights.

Respect Activity:

To further illustrate this point, break the participants into couples again, and perform this activity from Miller (2004) called "But Nothing (Feedback)." Here is how it works:

- Have the participants pair up into couples.
- Explain that each participant is to think of something about their partner's outfit that they like.
- Next, think of something that would make the outfit look better.
- Each participant takes a turn and tells their partner what they like, then say the word "but" and explain what would make the outfit better.
- Then, ask the question "How did you feel when your partner gave you a compliment followed by "but?" (Students will express feelings of anger, frustration, defensives and annoyance.)
- Then, ask how we could get the same point across in a better way.
- After taking suggestions, explain that we can replace the word "but" with the word "and."
- Have the students do the same activity replacing the word "but" with "and."

To close the activity, discuss the difference in how the participants felt, and discuss why we might use the word "but" so often when providing feedback. Students will often come to the conclusion it has to do with a leader feeling superior or that they are "in charge" and have the final say.

Effectiveness

The fifth building block to positive leadership is effectiveness. In this instance effectiveness of the leader, not the group is what is important. The success of the organization is a direct reflection of its leadership. So how can one increase the effectiveness of their leaders? Lautzenheiser (1993) comments that "It is important to remind our student leaders of the universal law of leadership: You can't lead others until you lead yourself" (p. 133). Leaders must set the example. They must be a constant source of appropriate and positive behavior. Lautzenheiser (1993) goes on to say "The performance of the group offstage will reflect the success of the group onstage, and much of this will be determined by the effectiveness of the student leaders" (p. 133).

If the goal of leadership is to unite members of an organization in reaching an objective, then this is the device by which we must measure our effectiveness. Boonshaft (2002) gives concrete thoughts on what one must do to ensure this. He says, "We must constantly encourage, positively reinforce, press for and require progress, growth, hard work, achievement, and concentration. We must never allow the focus of our work to venture away from our goals. We must apply firm but appropriate pressure toward that goal" (p. 128). Success will be inevitable if these guidelines are followed, thus the effectiveness of the group's leadership could never be brought into question.

Effectiveness Activity:

To further discuss effectiveness, have the participants again break into couples. Then begin this activity developed by Jackson (1995). The activity is simply called "Partners," and this is how it works:

- Once the participants are in pairs explain that they must accomplish a simple everyday task while holding one of their partner's hands.

- The partners may work together. One person does not have to accomplish the task on their own.
- Tasks can include folding a paper airplane, untie and tie a shoe, roll up a sheet of newspaper and put a rubber band around it, inflate and tie a balloon or any other activity you may want to come up with.

Then, discuss how effective each participant was at accomplishing these seemingly easy tasks. Ask them to draw parallels between this activity and what happens in our organization. People outside the organization often see what we do and think that it is an easy thing to do; like tying a shoe or blowing up a balloon. They often don't realize that there are other circumstances that we must deal with which can sometimes make what appears to be an easy task much more difficult. Discuss the following points as well:

- Would the task have been easier to accomplish without the help of your partner?
- What does this tell us about working as a team? (Sometimes we must do things for ourselves.)
- Have you ever been in a situation where the involvement of a group slowed you down?
- If frustration occurs when working with a group what can you do to lessen that frustration?

Trustworthiness

The term trustworthy has many synonyms. One will hear words like honesty, integrity and credibility. Whichever term is chosen, the definition remains the same-conducting oneself in a manner which lends itself to being trusted by others.

Lautzenheiser (2005) gives a list of personality traits to look for in student leaders. This is what he says about being honest. "Slighting the truth is commonplace. The student who avoids the temptation to exaggerate or embellish the truth and is willing to accept the consequences that often accompany honesty is a rare commodity. Everyone will benefit from being in the presence of a person who demonstrated such personal integrity" (p. 89).

Integrity or trust is very high on the priority list for effective leaders. After all, who would want to follow someone they don't trust? Maxwell (1993) states:

> The more credible you are the more confidence people place in you, thereby allowing you the privilege of influencing their lives. The less credible you are, the less confidence people place in you and the more quickly you lose your position of influence....As I have said time and time again, everything rises and falls on leadership. The secret to rising and not falling is integrity (p. 38).

Being trusted by the members of the organization goes hand-in-hand with the fourth principle of leadership, respect, which was discussed earlier. If one gains the trust of the group they have also gained their respect. Because respect is a two way street, the leader must now follow the previous guidelines and give respect in order to retain the respect of the group.

Trustworthiness Activity:

Demonstrate trust with a very common activity. It is called "The Trust Fall." Many of us have played this game in our youth, and in order to clarify the activity set it up for the participants as follows:

- Have groups of ten to twelve participants.
- Instruct one of the participants to stand on a raised platform (chair, small table, stump, etc.)
- The remaining members of the group stand in two lines behind the person on the platform. They are the spotters.
- Instruct the falling person (on the platform) to not bend their knees as they fall as this will cause the force to be concentrated on a couple of spotters.
- The spotters should stand facing each other with arms outstretched palms and forearms up.
- The falling person should cross their arms, announce when he/she is ready to fall and then fall straight back without bending their knees.
- Allow each participant to take a turn as the falling person.

Touch on the following discussion points to close out the activity:

- Was it harder to fall or catch? Why?
- How did it feel to be forced to rely on others?
- How does this relate to trust in our organization?
- The spotters were looking out for the falling person. Do we have an obligation in our organization to look out for each other?
- What are some of the ways that we "fall" in our organization?
- What can we do to help those who have fallen?
- The falling person had to rely on everyone else. Do we need to rely on each other in our organization? How?

Selflessness

The final component of effective positive leadership is the ability to be selfless. This is the most difficult trait to master and retain for leaders of all ages. Even adults have problems with this component. It is my estimation that this trait is so difficult to master because it requires an enormous amount of maturity. A discussion with students about maturity, or the lack of maturity, fits in very well here.

Books on the issue of leadership often refer to this principle as the ability to make a shift from what is called I-me mentality to we-us mentality. As a music director, one tries to encourage students to think about the ensemble, blending, unity, and working together, yet in many instances, directors will convey messages to the contrary without even knowing it. Lautzenheiser (1993) sums it up best when he says:

> Defensive actions, negative attitudes, fear of risk, avoidance of change, and stringent protective behavior all stem from insecurity and/or fear. They are behavioral postures we assume for self-protection. These defenses create walls and obstacles which prevent communication and cooperation, and strongly reinforce the I-me pattern of living, which is the antithesis of what we are striving to achieve in our musical community ("with unity"), opening the pathways to artistic experiences....The point is, as teachers, performers, conductors, and students, we must constantly discipline our own behavior so it aligns with our desires (p. 143-144).

Another way to encourage "we-us" situations is to look for what are called win/win solutions to problems. This means that when confronted with a problem the leader will try to find a solution where both parties agree on an outcome without harming the other party in any way. This is what Covey (1989) has to say about win/win situations:

Most people tend to think in terms of dichotomies: strong or weak, hardball or softball, win or lose. But that kind of thinking is fundamentally flawed. It's based on power and position rather than on principle. Win/Win is based on the paradigm that there is plenty for everybody, that one person's success is not achieved at the expense or exclusion of the success of others. Win/Win is a belief in the Third Alternative. It's not your way or my way; it's a better way, a higher way (p. 207).

The final activity comes from the video series by Dr Tim Lautzenheiser (2003).
- Tell the participants they will once again need to get into groups of two.
- Imagine that there is a bag of money between them which they are going to either put money into or take money out.
- The game is played much like rock, paper, scissors except that each participant throws only one finger or two.
- Explain it as follows:

"If you throw a one and your partner throws a two you put $3.00 in the bag (-$3.00) and your partner takes out $8.00 (+$8.00). If you throw a two and your partner tthrows a one you gain $8.00 (+$8.00) and your partner loses $3.00 (-$3.00). If you both throw a two you both lose $8.00 and if you both throw a one you both gain $2.00." Create a table as follows for the participants to follow:

Player One	Player Two
Throw a **One**: - $3.00	Throw a **Two**: + $8.00
Throw a **Two** : + $8.00	Throw a **One**: - $3.00
Throw a **Two**: - $8.00	Throw a **Two**: - $8.00
Throw a **One**: +$2.00	Throw a **One**: +$2.00

- Explain that there is no talking during this activity.
- Play ten rounds and students total their points after each round.
- Once ten rounds are completed, ask by a show of hands how many people have a positive number and then, how many have a negative number.
- Then ask if any group has both members holding a positive $20.00. If there are tell the participants to take a good look at these people because they are the leaders and friends you want to have.

- Take a close look at the chart with the participants. Go through each portion and point out that there is only one option on the chart that is a win-win situation. The only win-win is when both members throw a one.
- How is this activity also related to trust?

The leader who is able to make the shift from I-me to the we-us mentality and find win/win situations has already won the majority of the battle. Once the principle of selflessness is attained, the other six principles will fall into place rather easily.

It's All About The Shoes

After one workshop with students a young lady approached me and said, "It seems to me like you are not teaching us to be leaders. You are teaching us to conform." I asked her to take a look at my shoes. I was wearing a pair of shoes that are made of patches of various shade of purple leather. She commented that they were "really cool." I thanked her for the compliment and explained that in our society I must conform to the need for shoes. In fact, I said, "Look around. Everyone in this room is wearing shoes. Even you conformed to this one. We all conform to some extent."

Yes, I told her. I have to wear shoes, but I don't have to do it in the way that everyone else expects me to. I can do this my own way. People take notice of my shoes, but I'm not doing anything that is disrespectful, hurtful or negative in anyway. I went on to explain that I am known for my many shoes in crazy designs and patterns, and it has even inspired students in my very conservative and rural school district to emulate my style at school assemblies and on dress up days. Many students have even consulted me on getting outrageous shoes to wear for prom.

I went on to tell her that this is what I want from you as a leader. I have discussed ideas that are not new, and skills that all people possess. I want you to take these skills and ideas which are very ordinary and I want to make them extraordinary. I want you to use them to inspire others and create a better situation for you, your organization, your school and your community.

Discussion

This manual has dealt with seven principles of effective positive leadership. These principles were taken from several sources and synthesized into what I developed as the SECRETS of leadership with each principle representing one letter of the word "secrets." These principles are sensitivity, enthusiasm, communication, respect, effectiveness, trustworthiness and selflessness.

In completion of this project, and as discussed earlier, I actually put this manual to use, and created a leadership training day for my own students. The rewards were tremendous! My students seem to have more of an interest in what is happening with our program. They have developed a sense of ownership in this program, because they now understand their roles not only as members of the organization, but as leaders of the organization. They have come to realize that part of their responsibility as leaders is to serve, not to be served. This has lead to more students volunteering to stay late and help put equipment back in order, or complete other organizational tasks. I am looking forward to the future with my students to see how this develops in the coming years. I hope to develop a second series of activities or exercises to further aid in the development of our youth.

The job we have as music educators involves more than just teaching notes on a page or how to march. We as educators have the awesome responsibility to use music as a means by which to teach a student to be the best person he or she can be.

It is my sincere hope that you will take this manual and use the ideas in it as a stepping stone to creating your own leadership training classes, and in turn produce more positive and constructive students who will help to improve your organization, your school and your community.

In order to inspire our students to be great leaders, we must first teach ourselves to be great leaders. We must practice the "secrets" and reveal them in our daily lives. We should not only preach positive leadership, but we must also live it.

I will conclude with a quote by Lautzenheiser (1993). "We must constantly demand of ourselves what we expect of others. To improve our own conditions, we must embrace change instead of fear it, accept others and their insecurities, and love even those people who seem to disagree with our thoughts and feelings. This is not an end within itself, but an ongoing process" (p. 145).

References

Boonshaft, P.L., (2002). *Teaching music with passion: Conducting, rehearsing, and inspiring*. Galesville, MD: Meredith Music Publications.

Brinkman, R., & Kirschner, R., (2002). *Dealing with people you can't stand: How to bring out the best in people at their worst*. New York: McGraw-Hill.

Carnegie, D., (1936). *How to win friends & influence people* (Rev. ed.). New York: Pocket Books.

Covey, S. R., (1989). *The 7 habits of highly effective people: Powerful lessons in persona change*. New York: Free Press.

Goldman, E. F., (1916). *The amateur band guide and aid to leaders*. Chicago: Carl Fischer.

Jackson, T., (1993). *Activities That Teach*. Cedar City, UT: Red Rock Publishing.

Jackson, T. (1995). *More Activities That Teach*. Cedar City, UT: Red Rock Publishing.

Lautzenheiser, T., (1993). *The joy of inspired teaching*. Chicago: GIA Publications.

Lautzenheiser, T., (2005). *Music advocacy and student leadership: Key components of every successful music program*. Chicago: GIA Publications.

Maxwell, J. C., (1993). *Developing the leader within you*. Nashville, TN: Thomas Nelson.

Maxwell, J. C., (1998). *The 21 irrefutable laws of leadership: Follow them and people will follow you*. Nashville, TN: Thomas Nelson.

Miller, B.C., (2004). *Quick Team-Building Activities for Busy Managers*. New York: Amacom.

Mullins, S., (1985). *Teaching music: The human experience*. Yellow Springs, OH: Shirley Strohm Mullins.

Rathe, T., & Clifton, D. O., (2004). *How full is your bucket: Positive strategies for work and life*. New York: Gallup Press.

Rush, S., (2003). *Habits of a successful band director: Pitfalls and solutions*. Fort Wayne, IN: Focus On Excellence.

Additional References

Allen, R., (1985). *Let it begin with me.* Nashville, TN: Broadman Press.

Bennis, W. & Nanus, B., (1985). *Leaders.* New York: Harper & Row.

Biehl, B., (1989). *Increasing your leadership confidence.* Sisters: Questar Publishers.

Cook, W. H., (1974). *Success, motivation and the scriptures.* Nashville, TN: Broadman Press.

Dilenschneider, R., (1990). *Power and influence: Mastering the art of persuasion.* New York: Prentice Hall.

Drucker, P., (1974). *Management, tasks, responsibilities and practices.* New York: Harper & Row.

Fournies, F. F., (1978). *Coaching for improved work performance.* New York: Van Nostrand Reinhold.

Greenleaf, R. K., (1977). *The servant as leader.* Mahwah: Paulist.

Hartley-Leonard, D., (1987, August 24). Perspectives. *Newsweek,* 11.

Kouzes, J., & Posner, B., (1987). *The leadership challenge.* San Francisco, CA: Josey-Bass.

McKenzie, E. C., (1980). *Quips and quotes.* Grand Rapids, MI: Baker.

McKown, H. C., (1985). *A boy grows up.* New York: McGraw Hill.

Miller, J.R., (1975). *The building of character.* New Jersey: AMG Publishers.

Mohney, N. (1986, July 25). Beliefs can influence attitudes. *Kingsport Times News*, pp. 4B.

Morin, W. J., & Yorks, L., (1990). *Dismissal.* San Fancisco, CA: Harcourt Brace Jovanovich.

Peale, N. V., (1988). *Power of the plus factor.* New York: Fawcett.

Peters, T., & Waterman, R., (1984) *In search of excellence.* New York: Warner.

Robinson, D., (1990). Mind over Disease. *Reader's Digest, March 1990.*

Von Oech, R., (1986). *A kick in the seat of the pants.* San Francisco, CA: HarperCollins.

Waitley, D., & Witt, R. L., (1985). *The joy of working.* New York: Dodd, Mead, & Co.

www.ingramcontent.com/pod-product-compliance
Lightning Source LLC
Chambersburg PA
CBHW081238170526

45165CB00009B/3094